ONE SMALL KINDNESS

CAN CHANGE THE COURSE OF A LIFE

COMMENCEMENT ADDRESS BY

AMY WHITE

ISBN-10: 0-9960337-2-6
ISBN-13: 978-0-9960337-2-5

10 9 8 7 6 5 4 3 2 1   11 12 13 14 15 16 17
Printed in the U.S.A.
First softcover edition, May 2017

for
my kids
(all of them)

Rocky Mountain High School Graduation Ceremony
May 20, 2017
Moby Arena
Fort Collins, Colorado

ONE
SMALL
KINDNESS

Hi, you guys! You look so good in your caps and your gowns! You look so smart. All educated and ready for the real world.

And look at all these people!
They're here because of you!
They're here because they love you.
They're here because they're proud of
you. They're making me super nervous.
But they love you, and they're proud of
you. And I'm proud of you, too!

For some of you, this was a really long journey. For some of you it was easier, but it's no less satisfying to be here. Take a moment to appreciate it, to soak it in. Find your families, find your supporters, find your friends, find those people who were with you along this journey. Remember this time, because however you got here, it's a milestone. It's a rite of passage, and it means you're ready for the next step, whatever that might be.

It's exciting, and it's a special moment. So enjoy it!

I'm glad to share this moment with you. I appreciate your confidence in asking me to speak. That meant a lot to me. I don't know what you were thinking, but it means a lot to me to be asked. When I was trying to decide what to say, my husband suggested talking about the Broncos, because everybody likes them. But if you've had me in class you know I know nothing about the Broncos.

I'm going to talk about what I know about, and that's teaching — what I've learned from teaching and what I've learned from you.

First of all, if you've had me in class, you know that I didn't want to be a teacher. I wanted to go to law school. I was actually in law school, but I was engaged, and I really wanted to marry Jeff White. My parents helpfully suggested that one of us should get a job before we got married. He was still finishing school, and that left me.
I dropped out of law school, and I applied for a job teaching high school English. I didn't want to be a teacher but I had an English degree and that's what you do with an English degree, yes? Fortunately, they were desperate for teachers in Los Angeles back in 1990, and they gave me a job teaching 10th grade English.

This was back when we left kids behind, and we didn't require anyone to be highly qualified, so I was good! I did know English. I am highly qualified now, however, and I take them kicking and screaming. I do not leave any of them behind!

So I remember they offered me the job, and I called Jeff White and I said, "I got the job! I'm making $20,000 a year! We can get married!"

We thought we were rich!

And so we got married. I started school on a Monday. I got married that Saturday. My timing has always been very poor. But we were in love!

We were happy!

I liked teaching, but it was a temporary gig. I was going back to law school. But I was pretty okay at it. It was fun most days. It's still fun more days than it's not.

One of the more difficult days, however, was in January of my first year. We had gone to my grandma's house for my dad's birthday, and we discovered that my uncle had killed himself. We were devastated. It's one of those days that you never forget in your life.

It was a Thursday, and I had school the next day. And if you know me, you know I hate missing school. I didn't have that many days left and I thought, "It's okay, I'll go to school." We were starting a drama unit, and we were going to watch a play. So I thought, "I'll be okay."

I discovered after first hour that it was going to be a little more difficult than I had thought. I was rolling that big TV into the classroom (this was 1991 — you had to roll the big TV in with the big VCR), and the kids got super excited when they saw it coming, because that meant they're watching a video today. I was setting up the VCR and I kept pushing the tape in and it kept popping back out. I kept pushing the tape in and it kept popping back out. I was like, it's rewound, it's not tangled. (Do you remember those tapes? Have you ever seen those? They're in your basement.) But it kept popping back out and I did not know what to do. And I was starting to lose it, as we do over the tiny things that happen in life.

I remember a student walked up to me. His name was Eric. And he put his hand on my shoulder, and he said, "I've got this Miss White. You look like you need a minute."

I don't know if any other student noticed. If they did I didn't see it. But Eric did. I walked outside my classroom door and I cried. I cried because of his kindness. And I cried because of my loss. I don't know what made me cry more.

In that moment, I knew that there was no place I'd rather be than in that classroom. And I knew that there was no one I would rather be with than those kids. They were important and they were valuable. And they needed to know that.

So I walked back in, and through my tears I looked at every one of them, and I said, "You are so important, and you are so valuable." And I've said that to every class I've had since then. Because you guys are important. You are the only ones who can do what you do. And we need you! I need you!

There have been so many years since then that my kids have gotten me through. And you're all my kids! People think I have so many children when I talk about them. I have the ones that I birthed, but you guys are a lot better sometimes. (Sorry, he's up there — he's listening!)

You have no idea how much my students have meant to me over the years. Your small kindnesses to me and to others have been inspiring. I'm a better person because of you.

I know we hear about bullying, and I know it exists, absolutely. But what I've seen the most are amazing young people who are trying to change their world.

One small
kindness can
change the
course of a life.

It changed mine. I'm sure some of you could say the same.

Never forget that.

You can't make other people happy, but you can make them miserable. Choose kindness whenever you can.

I know it's not always easy to be kind.
I know that you get beat up sometimes
by the older generations who complain
that you are lazy, or not prepared for
the world. And while they may be right,
I can assure you that my generation
was equally lazy and equally unpre-
pared. And yet somehow we turned into
productive adults, with houses and jobs
and cars and stuff.

What makes you different from me
and my generation is that you know
so much more. Technology available to
you today allows you to discover more
about the world, and it shows in your
passions and in your pursuits.

I didn't know nearly as much about the world around me when I was your age. Nor did I care, frankly. I worked at a yogurt shop, and I flirted with boys. This was my life work. I was good at it.

It wasn't until college, when I went to South Africa, that I started to care about what was going on globally. And it wasn't until I met Jeff White that I started caring about things outside my small circle. He made me a better person, and he continues to make me a better person today.

Surround yourselves
with people who make you
better.

With people who encourage you to be
your best. And people who inspire and
challenge you to be better.

I know I'm probably not the best English teacher you've ever had, and I'm okay with that. But I show up every day, and every day I give my best.

I'm a better person because of you. I hope all of you will give your best, too — even on days when it's difficult.

Because there's going to be difficult days. There will be days when you want to give up. Days when even your best looks pretty pathetic.

I know these days, and I've known some this year. I've gotten through them because of you, and because I look for a lot of reasons to be thankful. I wake up every morning and I choose to be grateful, even when I don't feel like it. I have a bracelet that I wear that reminds me. (Today I'm also wearing my "Be Brave" bracelet! Because sometimes a girl needs two bracelets!) It reminds me even when I don't feel like it, because some days I need the reminder. Some days I struggle to find things.

But I remember to find joy in those little things, in small kindnesses shown to me, because they're always there.

If you've had me in class, I've tried to encourage you to do that, too — to show gratitude. Because when you show gratitude, it literally makes you feel better. (And that is research based — look it up!)

I'm cheerful in the halls because I'm thankful to be at Rocky. I'm thankful to spend time with all of you. Sometimes I start my day out less than thankful, maybe on the drive to school or in the parking lot (because the parking lot is rough! Thank you all for not hitting me out there!). But by the time I walk through the halls I say, "Hello! Good morning! Happy Monday!" (How many of you have heard me say that?) I see your faces and I'm cheerful. I really am. I believe it's going to be a great day, and I'm grateful for it.

On your darkest days, think of something or someone that makes you thankful. If you can, call them, text them, tell them that you're thankful for them today. Because then you've made them happy, too.

I woke up this morning and I was nervous. I don't get nervous much. That's a new feeling for me. But I remembered that I am thankful for all of you. I'm thankful that I get to be a part of this moment with you. And somehow I got here and I don't think I've totally screwed this up. (That doesn't mean you need to ask again — it seemed like such a better idea in November than it did

Thank you for sharing your day with me. And for some of you — you know who you are — thank you for sharing your lives with me. Thank you for sharing your story. And thank you for being a part of my life. I'm excited to see where life takes you, and what the future holds for you.

So when you go out there into the real world, the world you've heard so much about, remember to be kind. The world won't always be kind to you, but do your best to be kind back. Because people are important.

You are important.

Find those people who believe that, too, and who make you better. Seek them, search them out, and be the very best person possible. And never forget to say "Thank you" along the way — for the small things, and for the big things.

I believe that we are living in exciting times. And I hope you will live your life like you believe that, too.

Congratulations!

SMALL KINDNESSES I CAN DO

SMALL KINDNESSES I CAN DO

_____

_____

_____

_____

_____

_____

_____

_____

_____

_____

KIND THINGS I CAN SAY

_____

_____

_____

_____

_____

_____

_____

_____

_____

_____

KIND THINGS I CAN SAY

_____

_____

_____

_____

_____

_____

_____

_____

_____

_____

KIND GIFTS I CAN GIVE

KIND GIFTS I CAN GIVE

_____

_____

_____

_____

_____

_____

_____

_____

_____

_____

PEOPLE I AM THANKFUL FOR

PEOPLE I AM THANKFUL FOR

_____

_____

_____

_____

_____

_____

_____

_____

_____

_____

THINGS I AM THANKFUL FOR

THINGS I AM THANKFUL FOR

_____

_____

_____

_____

_____

_____

_____

_____

_____

_____

REASONS I AM IMPORTANT

REASONS I AM IMPORTANT

_____

_____

_____

_____

_____

_____

_____

_____

_____

_____

PEOPLE WHO MAKE ME BETTER

PEOPLE WHO MAKE ME BETTER

_____

_____

_____

_____

_____

_____

_____

_____

_____

_____

PEOPLE WHO LOVE ME

PEOPLE WHO LOVE ME

PLACES I WANT TO GO

PLACES I WANT TO GO

THINGS I WANT TO DO

THINGS I WANT TO DO

STUFF I WANT TO LEARN

STUFF I WANT TO LEARN

THINGS I DON'T WANT TO FORGET

THINGS I DON'T WANT TO FORGET

LITTLE THINGS THAT GIVE ME JOY

LITTLE THINGS THAT GIVE ME JOY

_____

_____

_____

_____

_____

_____

_____

_____

_____

HOW TO HAVE A HAPPY MONDAY

_____

_____

_____

_____

_____

_____

_____

_____

_____

_____

_____

HOW TO HAVE A HAPPY MONDAY

_____

_____

_____

_____

_____

_____

_____

_____

_____

_____

Amy White is a high school English teacher at Rocky Mountain High School in Fort Collins, Colorado. She also teaches painting classes on the weekends. She's been to five continents, has two masters degrees, and has a chow chow named Princess Pow Pow. Amy and her husband Jeff have three children: Luke, Daisy, and Cooper.